Five Star God © 2018 by Ginae Lee Scott

All rights reserved. No part of this publication may be reproduced, distributed, or transmitted in any form or by any means, including photocopying, recording, or other electronic or mechanical methods, without the prior written permission of the publisher or author, except in the case of brief quotations embodied in critical reviews and certain other noncommercial uses permitted by copyright law. For permission requests, email the publisher or author at addresses below:

Contact the author:
www.ginaeleescott.com | instagram @artistginae

Contact the publisher:
Unprecedented Press LLC - 495 Sleepy Hollow Ln, Holland, MI 49423
www.unprecedentedpress.com | info@unprecedentedpress.com
twitter: @UnprecdntdPress | instagram: unprecedentedpress

Scripture taken from the New King James Version®. Copyright © 1982 by Thomas Nelson. Used by permission. All rights reserved.

Scripture quotations from The Authorized (King James) Version. Rights in the Authorized Version in the United Kingdom are vested in the Crown. Reproduced by permission of the Crown's patentee, Cambridge University Press

ISBN-13: 978-1-7321964-2-1
ISBN-10: 1-7321964-2-7

Printed in the United States of America
Ingram Printing & Distribution, 2018

Edited by Margo Dill

First Edition

Unprecedented
Press

*How your life
can reflect
His lavish light*

GINAE LEE SCOTT

table of contents

Dedication	1
1 - What is Five Star?	3
2 - What Five Star is Not	11
3 - Expectations	19
4 - What Do We Deserve?	27
5 - Accepting God's Love in Peace	43
6 - What Can Hinder Our Five Star Life?	51
7 - Why Does God Want to Bless Us?	61
8 - How Do I Find the Five Star God?	71
9 - Will God Be a Five Star God to Me?	81
10 - Who Can Keep Us from Our Five Star God?	91
11 - It's Day by Day	103
From the Author	123
About the Author	125
Everyone Global Giving	127
Other Titles	128

*This book is dedicated to Rosa Julie,
a wonderful woman full of faith,
whom I met on the beaches of Anguilla.*

1
what is five star?

When we hear "Five Star," our minds usually go to something we consider elite, something grand—an awesome hotel we've heard about, complete with white sand beaches and turquoise waters surrounding it. A staff will wait on our every need and will bring us some of those cute, drinks with umbrellas in them. Or we picture the resort someone we know recently vacationed at, and it looked wonderful to us from their Facebook photos, and we hope one some day we can get there also. Five Star always looks like a take-us-away place, a place where all is good and everything is perfect. And if we've ever been fortunate enough, we can go back in our own memories to the Five Star resort we've vacationed at and we reminisce about the wonderful times we've had and wish we could go back…like, yesterday.

Five Star God

Five Star is a rating used by reviewers to help us consumers when looking for hotels to stay in, movies to go to, restaurants to eat at, TV shows to watch, cars that are safe to drive, medical centers and nursing homes for our loved ones, and the list goes on and on. The average person would feel safe eating or staying at a four to five star rated restaurant or hotel. A lot of us would love to even afford eating at Five Star restaurants and vacationing in Five Star hotels—those kind of ratings can often make a person feel like they have "arrived", and they are getting the best there is to offer in life.

A Five Star hotel can make a person expect a lot more when staying as a guest than a lesser rated hotel. We would expect better overall treatment, cleaner rooms, a courteous staff, and all the extras—like our beds turned down in the evening with those little after dinner mints placed on our pillowcases. A bathrobe, slippers, and the special soaps in the bathroom are also a wonderful addition and treat with the Five Star hotels. My favorite is the Keurig coffee pot that is in some of the higher rated hotels. And of course, they have included every special coffee and tea imaginable at our disposal. Yes, Five Star can be awesome, expensive, and sometimes out of our reach. Five Star can mean superior over the others in their class. Five Star is the top rating.

Superior – Higher in rank, status, quality, further above, higher in position, first rate, excellent, first choice, select, top-choice, first-class, prime, upscale, worthier, prize, and Five Star.

Five Star – The highest quality, the best there is, used to measure luxury, first-class, and above the rest.

Now, we've gone over the basics of a Five Star rating—it's the best of the best. It's luxury above anything that we are used to. It's the prime of the prime. It's higher in position than others. The quality is above all others. It's first choice. It's worthy. It's a prize above all others.

Prime – First importance, the main, excellent, the best possible quality, vigor, a length of time of greatest strength.

While acknowledging all of this information about a Five Star rating, we could agree that Five Star sounds pretty good. Five Star sounds above the rest. We would want to reach for Five Star because that is the best—the prime of the prime, so to speak. What would we say if we were told that most of us never reach for the Five Star that is available to us? How could we reach for a Five Star of anything, if we didn't know it existed in the first place? A lot of us can't even imagine a Five Star of anything. What would we think if we believed what we were told—that our

God has no limits, we cannot measure Him with our rulers, and God's equations do not make sense in our math?

God's Equations Don't Measure Up

John 6 - Seven loaves of bread feeds 5,000 with 12 baskets of bread left over? How does that happen? How do we end up with more than what we started with?

II Peter 3:8 - One day is a thousand days; a thousand days is a day. How do we figure that out? A thousand days cannot fit into a day, and one day cannot stretch out to a thousand days on our calendar.

Exodus 20:11 – He created the world in six days and rested on the seventh. How does something this big get created in six days and spoken into existence? No way by our calculations.

What would we say if we were shown all the Five Star situations that we missed out on because we weren't looking for them, nor did we expect them? If a huge projector started right now on the wall before us, and the screen replayed all the missed Five Star blessings that we left behind because we didn't know they were for us, what would we say? What would we think? What would we do?

If the Lord is a Five Star God, then we have to wonder: does He want a Five Star life for us? What is a Five Star life with the Lord? That is the goal to find out. By the end of this book, we should know more about the Five Star life that God truly wants for us. With that knowledge, we should be more open to His plans for us, and we should be reaching higher in Him than we have ever imagined. A Five Star life is what He wants for us because He is a Five Star God!

> *But thou shalt remember the Lord thy God; for it is He that giveth thee power to get wealth, that He may establish His covenant, which He swore unto thy fathers, as it is this day.*
> *~ Deuteronomy 8:18*

> *And this same God who takes care of me will supply all your needs from his glorious riches, which have been given to us in Christ Jesus. ~ Philippians 4:19*

> *Therefore do not worry, saying, "What shall we eat?" or "What shall we drink?" or "What shall we wear?" For after all these things the Gentiles seek. For your heavenly Father knows that you need all these things. But seek first the kingdom of God and His righteousness, and all these things shall be added to you.*
> *~ Matthew 6:31-33*

> *The Lord is my shepherd, I shall not want. ~ Psalm 23:1*

> **God's measurements are not our measurements.**
> **So what are His?**
> **God's expectations are not our expectations.**
> **So what are His?**
> **God's thoughts are not our thoughts.**
> **So what are His?**

God is superior and is above anything we can imagine. From His vantage point, He sees from the secret place of the holiness of God. Jesus emphasized that His vantage point is above this world. We will need to learn to understand and see from Jesus and try to get a glimpse from His vantage point. When we get to know the Lord and grow in Him, we will look at things differently than we did before; that is a guarantee. And I love a guarantee, don't you? When we get to know our Five Star God better, we will find out His expectations and thoughts for us are above anything we could have ever hoped for or imagined.

Vantage point - a way of thinking about things that comes from our own particular situation or experiences—a good position from which we can see something.

Reflection Questions –

What is the Five Star rating?

Do you look for a Five Star life?

Does God measure by our measurements?

2

what five star is not

Our minds can travel all over the place when we talk about a Five Star rating. The oohs and ahhs can register in our imagination in seconds. Some of us, with a more vivid imagination, can really take our examples of the Five Star rating to an extreme. Fun though, isn't it? Going to the great beyond in our expectations, dreams, and imagination is really a good gift to have, so don't squelch it. I believe we need the big dreamers to help some of us that aren't dreaming big enough. We do need to think outside the box and that typically means 'bigger.' We need to think big. Dreamers, and the really big dreamers in God, usually see more things happening in their lives than someone who doesn't dream at all—due to the fact that unless we look for something, we probably won't find it.

In this chapter, let's explore what the Five Star rating is not. In chapter one, we read about the basic examples of the reviewer's work for the consumer and the Five Star rating definition. We know that a Five Star rating is superior above the rest. We know in the business world that businesses take pride in reaching such a goal. By reaching the highest rating of Five Star, it is also very good for their continued success in business.

We just touched on if God is a Five Star God, then does He want a Five Star life for us? This book is one hundred percent about bringing us to a place of knowledge that the Lord does want Five Star for us in everything. We are His children, and He loves us beyond anything we can imagine. We will explore in the next chapters how we can expect and accept His Five Star blessings; however before we do, let's explore what Five Star is not, so we don't go off in the wrong direction while receiving this knowledge. This thought of being blessed may be new to us also; so, never having explored this thought, it may take us a while to understand and accept this from God. Our religion or traditions could have us thinking something totally different about God, if that is the case, unlearning and relearning what our minds have been trained to see and do takes time. Give yourself that time—God has all the time in the world, and He understands and loves us better than anyone.

It is in my opinion and my experience that the Five Star blessings that God has for us are not in the following:

just a gain for me-for me-for me type attitude. It's not in rubbing, praying over, and blessing a lottery ticket so we have the winning lottery numbers every weekend. It's not in the gimme, gimme type bad behavior. We can't whine and beg for it. We can't kick, scream, and throw a tantrum like a two year old and expect to get our way with the Five Star blessings, either. It's not all about us; it's not about self, and it won't make everything perfect in life.

We don't want to be shallow in our relationship with God. We don't want to approach our heavenly Father as the genie in the bottle, but we do want a sincere relationship with our heavenly Father who will take care of our every need, above and beyond our expectations.

A "pray and win everything we can desire" mentality is not what this book is about. We are not talking about a materialistic world mentality here—a love and lust for things, for trips, for money, for position and greed. We will be blessed with those things, we will be taken care of, and our lives can be superior, prime, and excellent with the right attitude in the Lord. That attitude is knowing it is about Him. He takes care of us. It is one hundred percent about Him.

Five Star is not gain without God. We cannot expect to wish, hope, and pray for things without God.

> *I am the vine; you are the branches. He who abides in Me, and I in him, bears much fruit; for without Me, you can do nothing.* ~ John 15:5

Without God - on our own, trusting in what we can do by the arm of our flesh, trying to make something happen by any means possible, and lacking. Without also means on the outside—on the outside of God.

For a Five Star life, we do not want to seek what we need by trusting in ourselves only to provide. We do not want to go forth in anything without God. We do not want God on the outside of our plans and dreams—looking in. And we do not want to be on the outside of the great plans He has for our lives, looking back at what we missed.

Gain without God could keep us lacking. Lacking is not living to the full potential that God has for us. Lacking is not Five Star.

We do not want to compare our lives to others, nor should we hold God to what we think He has blessed others with. A simple example would be a neighbor just bought a new car, and our car keeps breaking down. Been there? Our car is in the shop more than it is out. The bills are piling up from all the repairs and we find ourselves in a rental car at a ridiculous price per day, while our neighbors are pulling in and out of their driveway with a car in mint condition. This is when we don't need to get upset, doubt, and compare our lives with others. Can we imagine the shouting to the heavens that can happen in these types of situations? Yes, we all can imagine and maybe even remember some of our own personal rantings in these types of situations.

Comparing can really mess a person up here. Our thoughts when this happens can rage out of control: Why do they get a brand new car, and we're still trying to find enough money to get ours out of the shop? I've never had a new car, why? God, where are you? Do you love me? God, do you even know who I am?

We do not know the true circumstances if the above example is an actual situation, nor will we ever understand or know the truth of the situation with the attitude of: "Why me and not them? Why them and not me?" God could be doing for us right at that moment something awesome, and we are so busy suffering that we have no idea if something good is going on around us. We could really miss out on some awesome things in life because we are comparing, and our eyes are closed to the real story.

We may see others always blessed, and our prayers go unanswered. Why is that, we ask ourselves, and then the sinking feeling weighs us down—and we think: is it me? This seems to happen to many people, and the enemy of our soul can use what we see happening for others against us.

When these questioning emotions come up, on top of us questioning what's going on in our lives, the average person will also feel bad about having these comparing emotions. We don't want to feel jealous or bad for someone else's blessings, but we do. The battle now becomes bigger. Then we question if it is just us. We begin to think: this doesn't happen to everyone, and then we isolate ourselves in those thoughts. And then we really start to question if God loves us.

Keeping our eyes on others is not a good road to choose. With God, the best plan is to keep our eyes on Him and what He is doing in our lives. This discipline or learned behavior does not come easy. It is something we need to make a conscious effort to do daily. Our journey with God is for the long haul. We won't learn how to have a great relationship with Him in a day; it will take a lifetime. Remember, we are learning, we are growing, and we are developing our relationship with the Lord. We will cover how to put it all in His hands in later chapters. In these early chapters, we are preparing ourselves—for some of us, to be open to think differently, to see God better, to learn more and be open to His blessings.

God is a Five Star God, and He wants the best for His children. He's got this, and by being His children, we can, too. When we truly grasp this, it takes all the pressure off of us. It's all Him and Him alone. When He takes care of us, it comes with peace. Our pride does not have to rear its ugly head because our pride should have nothing to do with it. We can be prideful, and that usually is a good indicator that we are off on our own. So again, letting Him takes the pressure off of us. It's not a "giving up" either; it's walking with a friend whom you know cares, and it's a liberty to know it will go well, and we are taken care of. It's truly being set free.

Stand fast therefore in the liberty by which Christ has made us free, and do not be entangled again with a yoke of bondage. ~ Galatians 5:1

But let each one examine his own work, and then he will have rejoicing in himself alone, and not in another. ~ Galatians 6:4

For we dare not class ourselves or compare ourselves with those who commend themselves. But they, measuring themselves by themselves, and comparing themselves among themselves, are not wise. ~ 2 Corinthians 10:12

Reflection Questions –

What is the Five Star not?

How do we compare ourselves to others?

How do we not fall into the trap of comparing?

3

expectations

Have we ever asked ourselves what are our expectations of God are? Most of us may have reflected on what His expectations are in us, and that can bring up all the areas we think we fall short in. We think of all the disappointments we must be to Him. Rarely, do these thoughts bring up good things in our minds. Most of us don't want to even think about the word "expectation" because we believe it can't be good.

When I was doing my research and interviewing people about this subject, almost one hundred percent of the time the answer was the same: they never thought of their expectations in God. Those interviewed were always focused on what they thought His expectations were of them. And their thoughts made them feel that they always fell short, they didn't deserve anything, and they were a disappointment to Him, feeling guilt and shame.

This doesn't sound like a good way to walk around, does it? If we are to have life abundantly, then why does the average person walk around with such guilt and shame? When we are to stir up our most holy faith, believing in the creator of heaven and earth, and by the faith the size of a mustard seed, we can move mountains—is guilt and shame the way we should walk around? I'm not feeling it. I'm thinking there's something big we are missing.

So, back to the real question: what are our expectations in God and what are His expectations for us? Examining these two questions and keeping them in mind while reading this book will help us stay open to what God truly has for us. Sometimes the key element that is so important to our day is not even thought about, let alone examined enough, to have our answer.

When we think about an expectation in something, is it our habit to look too high in the range of expectations, and then we set ourselves up to always fall short? Or is it our habit to look way too low in our expected expectations and not do or get anything? For some of us, could our life experiences have already been more than challenging and disappointing, to say the least, that we aren't expecting anything anymore? Do we have a low self-esteem that keeps us looking at the floor, and even lower, in all our expectations? Or do we have expectations in everything and everyone to such high extremes that nothing can impress us and nothing measures up? Both extremes will make our lives miserable and not much in the Five Star expectation department will be happening for us.

All of us can fall in one of these examples in the middle, or we can swing, depending on the situation and moods in our lives, between low expectations or out of reach expectations. Either way, we are missing it. We all need a balanced healthy look at what our expectations should be, and where they should be coming from. We need to get to the place where we aren't swinging high, then low; but we have a consistent, straight ahead view of the expectations for our lives. In later chapters, we will discuss how we go about getting to that balanced place.

Expectation – The act or state of expecting, the belief that something will happen, anticipation, expecting, looking forward to, we will achieve something, and degree of probability.

After reading the definition of expectation, it sounds a lot like the word faith. Faith and expectation are two completely different things; however if working with God, they work together in a balanced way and will actually work together— meaning that our faith is in God, and our expectations can be our miracle ground. When our expectations in life are open to what God may have for us, want from us, and have planned for us, then mixed with a faith that all is in God and from God, watch out! Five Star blessings are about to happen. It takes a load off knowing, it's not us that has to make something happen—it's Him. When we truly grasp this and walk in this truth, things will begin to happen.

Faith - Strong or unshakeable belief in something, especially without proof or evidence, indeed, really. A trust in God, His purpose and actions.

Faith mixed with expectations, and expectations mixed with faith sounds like the Five Star secret. We can have faith in something so unshakeable, no proof or evidence is needed; and we can trust completely that the expectations we believe in are going to happen. The probability and anticipation knowing He is doing it for us, and we don't have to do one thing for His love and Five Star blessing is the best kind of expectation. And the best kind of faith!

Are we still asking what does God expect from us? Do we still fight that thought in our minds? He actually doesn't expect anything from us; that's what's so liberating. He loves us and wants to be there for US! To have that, we need to know He's there and start a relationship with Him. He will show us in His word and in our relationship with Him, the path and turns we are to take to grow in him. Don't think on the past rules you've learned, focus on Him. He will show you the way to go.

For those of us who haven't had a relationship with God, our minds may be going off in all kinds of directions mixed with fear. "Will I have to go to church?" "Will I have to change?" "How can I do this?" Take a moment and look at those questions. They are all about us again. They are about us not measuring up and not knowing what to do to be accepted.

Not to be redundant, but this needs to be said again, and again—it's about Him. He died for us and has an everlasting love for us. Let's give Him a moment to be there for us. Just that. Find Him, and He will show us the way. If there's something He wants for our good, He will show us and open the path to that direction. Relationship first, spend time with Him and the Five Star life will follow!

Let me point out here for those of us who are locked into that thought of "we must have to do something"—in God's word, we see the people before us who had a relationship with God that their faith caused them to do something we call works. Faith without works is dead; works without faith is dead, also. That said, in a relationship, we will do things to make that relationship better, but you must first have the relationship. We can't make a relationship better before we have it. We can't get perfect for the relationship before we have it either.

We can all fret before relationships' start to the point that we don't start the relationship. When wanting friendships, we can't stress over what it will cost to the point we sabotage every friendship. This is a good moment to look inside and see what we do in this situation and be very honest with ourselves. How we act in the natural is a good indication of how we can be with God in the spirit. Don't be hard on yourself if you see some traits you would rather not have; you are not alone. Remember, relationship first.

But those who hope in the Lord will renew their strength. They will soar on the wings like eagles; they will run and not grow weary; they will walk and not be faint. ~ Isaiah 40:31

Trust in the Lord with all your heart and lean not on your own understanding; in all your ways submit to Him, and He will make your paths straight. ~ Proverbs 3:5-6

But you, Lord, are a compassionate and gracious God, slow to anger, abounding in love and faithfulness. ~ Psalms 86:15

Do not be anxious about anything, but in every situation, by prayer and petition, with thanksgiving, present your requests to God. And the peace of God, which transcends all understanding, will guard your hearts and your minds in Christ Jesus. ~ Philippians 4:6-7

The righteous cry out, and the Lord hears, and delivers them out of all their troubles. The Lord is near to those who have a broken heart, and saves such as have a contrite spirit. Many are the afflictions of the righteous, But the Lord delivers him out of them all. ~ Psalms 34:17-19

Reflection Questions –

What are our expectations of God?

Does God expect from us?

Do we swing to an extreme in our expectations?

4

what do we deserve?

When we stop and think about the word deserve, what pops up in our mind? Deserve. Hmmm. Does that stir up nervousness? Does it stir up anger? This is another word we need to understand what we think it means, according to our lives. We need to see how we feel about the word, and our interpretation of it, when we apply it to our lives and our relationship with God.

Deserve - To be entitled of, worthy of merit, to qualify for, to have claim to, earn, reward or punishment.

After interviewing several people about receiving blessings from God and the word deserve, I wasn't shocked with the outcome. I wished the outcome was different, but it did not surprise me after feeling led to write this book. Most people brought up deserve before I could. In their opinion, when I asked if they received from a giving God, they didn't think they deserved something good from God. And if they had received what they considered blessings in the past, they had trouble accepting them, due to the fact they did not know if they deserved them. The word deserve was used almost 100% before I could say it. That outcome saddened me. A lot of us are walking around with shame and guilt, over our past or present lives, and not believing we deserve anything good from God—when forgiveness and complete freedom are waiting for us in Christ Jesus.

Stand fast therefore in the liberty by which Christ has made us free, and do not be entangled again with a yoke of bondage.
~ Galatians 5:1

Therefore if the Son makes you free, you shall be free indeed.
~ John 8:36

There is therefore now no condemnation to those who are in Christ Jesus, who do not walk according to the flesh, but according to the Spirit. For the law of the Spirit of life in Christ Jesus has made me free from the law of sin and death. For what the law could not do in that it was weak through the flesh, God did by sending His own Son in the likeness of sinful flesh, on account of sin: He condemned sin in the flesh, that the righteous requirement of the law might be fulfilled in us who do not walk according to the flesh but according to the Spirit.
~ Romans 8:1-4

For by grace you have been saved through faith, and that not of yourselves; it is the gift of God. *~ Ephesians 2:8*

The key to the word deserve is we don't deserve anything. Let that sink in a moment. We don't deserve anything, and there's nothing more we can do to deserve. Some of us right now will be saying, "See, I knew I was right. I don't deserve and will never be good enough to deserve." And that sort of thinking makes us want to throw the towel in and give up.

The key to deserve with God is opposite of what we think: we don't deserve anything, and there is nothing more we can do to deserve because it is not about us—it's all about Him. He thinks we deserve His forgiveness, love, and blessings. The Lord is our heavenly Father and wants to take care of us. He wants us to have Five Star blessings.

We don't deserve anything, and there's nothing more we can do to deserve. He thinks we deserve.

Let's try to let this sink in real good. I repeat, it's all about Him. He thinks we should have life abundantly. He wants to give it to us, and He loves us with a neverending love. All good and everything is from above. We don't have to become someone else. We don't have to be something we are not. We don't have to be some super, perfect, non-human machine to get Him to love us more. We don't have a ruler we have to measure up to. If we are His child, if we know He is our God and Savior, then it truly is not us at all—it is all Him—in everything! This could and should take the pressure off of us if will we let it.

If we could have the confidence and peace in the fact that yes, we don't deserve it, but He wants us to have it, how could that change our lives and how we look at Him, our lives and the outcome? If we could believe the Word of God in such a way to have a true, open relationship with Him, doing His will in our lives and accepting we are forgiven and truly His children, what would that be like? This may be a great time to write down what this could mean to us.

There are, of course, things we each feel we should do to become a child of the Lord. The Scriptures are clear on it; I think we've added so many legalistic things to our beliefs that we are confused at times. And where there is envy, strife and confusion, there is every evil work. We are not to be confused. We are to believe in Jesus—He is the way, the truth, and the life. As Believers, we become His child; and as His child, He wants the best for us. It's that simple.

> *But God demonstrates His own love toward us, in that while we were still sinners, Christ died for us.*
> *~ Romans 5:6*

> *For where envy and self-seeking exist, confusion and every evil thing are there.*
> *~ James 3:16*

The journey with God is not pain-free, perfect, or a utopia-type feeling every day. As His children, we will still live, have life here in this world, which will mean not everything is perfect. That still doesn't mean that through it all—all the life experiences and all the life lessons—He doesn't want the Five Star blessings for us. He is unlimited for us; He gives freely and wants us to believe that. As His children, He will take us places to show who we are and who He is. Saying that can evoke fear in some of us; we may think He has to take us to bad places, or our lessons will be hard, and punishment will be the journey. Sometimes, that is exactly what it feels like if we are realistic, and sometimes, that is exactly what it is because we may have put ourselves in situations that aren't for our good. Those will be an opportunities for the Lord to show us something. Whatever situation we are in, we must remember He is with us. No matter the situation, let it be a Five Star blessing, be open to what He is doing, expect His love, and see what happens!

There will be days and situations that just won't work out to what we think would be to our advantage or make life easier. Those are the days I think my faith is lower than my "everything is perfect" days. That's when our faith is or can be attacked. God is not a lesser God on those days. He's still with us, but that is when we can doubt and wonder. If the enemy of our souls is involved, then we can really get confused about what is going on and be fearful. When we get into those situations, that is when we need to take a deep breath and spend some time with God. Let Him show us what may be going on, and if the situation is not explained to us, then we need to trust in Him that it is still working together for our good. This is the time that is not especially easy, but also not worth losing sleep over knowing He's got this.

There are times in our lives we sit by the phone, so to speak, waiting to find something out…in trying times, we need to sit by God and wait for the call of knowledge. His word tells us that those who seek wisdom will get wisdom!

> *If any of you lacks wisdom, let him ask of God, who gives to all liberally and without reproach, and it will be given to him. But let him ask in faith, with no doubting, for he who doubts is like a wave of the sea driven and tossed by the wind.*
> *~ James 1:5-6*

Let's go over the key to deserve one more time because it is essential we get this. The key to deserve is we don't deserve. Say that … we don't deserve. How does that feel? We can't do anything in works or anything else our mind is trying to figure out to get God to love us more. We don't deserve, but He wants us to have His love. How does that feel? We may not be good at accepting His gifts, but He wants us to have them. We may want to avoid this even right now reading this, but He wants to give it to us. He doesn't want His love for us judged on whether or not we deserve it. He wants to freely give to us, His children.

This is not easy is it? I personally had a hard time with this, and I'm still learning. But I have a better grip on it because of His love for me. Each of us reading this book will probably need a better grip on this thought, too. It could be why we're reading this book. Remember it's not His problem; we may have a problem with receiving His blessings, but the problem is not the Lord. He wants to give us Five Star blessings.

I want to share a true story that I believe was the first step to writing this book. I was in Las Vegas with my daughter for a long weekend. Going back a little here, she wanted to take me on a weekend trip and also pay for it. I had a problem with that, and at first said no. I didn't want her to spend her hard earned money on me; but after saying no; however I could see I disappointed her big time by not accepting her gift. That was the first time I believe I heard God's voice on this subject. I felt really bad that I had said no to my daughter. Why couldn't I have just said yes and been pleased that she wanted to do this for me? I will get to that later.

After arriving in Las Vegas, we didn't do a lot of gambling, so our planned activities during the day were to tour all the hotels and stay at the pool. We planned on doing one half of the Las Vegas strip on the first day and then the other half the following day. At the first hotel, we looked up at the high ceilings, and we were amazed at the stores, and how beautiful everything was. Not wanting to shop, we ignored all the salespeople that were giving out free samples of the cosmetics, perfumes, and skincare items that their stores sold. We really weren't in the mood for shopping and didn't want to be bothered. We were on a mission and just wanted to tour the inside of the hotels.

A man walked up to us after we had turned down several other salespeople, and he was very persistent with me about my skincare, asking a lot of questions. He was very complimentary and kept saying that I had great skin and needed to take care of my skin for the future. He wanted me to try this beautiful bottled lotion from the country of Israel, made with ingredients from the Dead Sea. He was dressed differently from the other salespeople as he was in a suit and tie. On top of that, he was very distinguished looking. We wondered if he was the manager or owner. We both tried to get away from him, all the while he was asking us into the store.

Due to him being so persistent, we gave up and followed him into the most beautiful store that specialized in only skincare products. He went on about the products, showed me a few to try on my wrist; and after a while, I told him he was a very good salesman and that I would buy from him if I was going to purchase anything, but I wasn't. He gave me a funny look and said, "You think I'm a good salesman?"

At that moment, I realized I had made a mistake of some kind. I had no idea what, but I don't think he was a salesman for the store. But he wasn't offended either; it was almost as if I had complimented him. He began packaging up several different skincare items, placing them into a very beautiful shopping bag, and asked me to follow him to the cash register. He started ringing up all of these skincare beauty items, totaling up to an amount close to one thousand dollars. I kept looking at my daughter; my eyes were asking her, "What is happening here?"

After telling him 'thank you, we are leaving now, and I will take a brochure,' he asked me to wait. He then took a very large wad of one hundred dollar bills out of his suitcoat pocket. He peeled off several hundred dollar bills and handed them to me. He told me to take them and then hand them back to him. I did so, wanting to question what in the world was going on, but I kept my mouth shut for the moment. As I watched him put all the one hundred dollar bills in the register, then take some change back, sliding that into his side suit pocket I said, "Ahh... you can ask my daughter, I don't accept gifts well, but thank you, I'll be leaving now... and seriously, I will check this product out online when I get home."

He looked up at me and said in a very kind, controlled voice, "It's not my problem that you do not accept gifts well. I am giving this to you today." His attitude was solid, and it said, "Period, end of story." Then he proceeded to come around the register area, with the bag full of very expensive products, handed them to me, and put his hand on my shoulder and lightly pushed me out of the store saying, "Be blessed."

My daughter and I walked out of the store in a daze. I didn't get it. I still don't get it. What was that about? Why did he do that? Why had he never even considered my daughter or offered her products? She is absolutely beautiful, and the products would have been wonderful for her, too. We had so many questions running through our minds at fifty miles an hour.

One thing was for certain: what he said to me near the end of our visit, I knew, and so did my daughter, that it was from above. It was the Lord speaking to me. We continued to walk out of the building in a daze. I wanted to look back, but I couldn't. I had wondered if I had dreamt it, but I had my daughter and the heavy bag full of over one thousand dollars in skincare and beauty products as a witness to me that it had all just taken place.

I pondered for many months after what he said to me. "It's not my problem you do not accept gifts well. I am giving this to you today." Well, that one sentence changed my life. It was definitely a God moment. I had missed it totally being God, when I felt conviction over my daughter's offer of the trip, and I had said no at first. I really felt like God had corrected me at that time for my daughter's feelings, and that may have been part of it, but the rest was for me.

Why wouldn't I have just accepted such a nice gift? She had told me that I had always done things for her, and with her income tax refund, she wanted to do something for me.

Well, the why has been revealed to me, and that is the purpose of this book. It's what we've been reading in this chapter. We will cover more on this subject in the next chapter—part of the why is we feel we don't deserve. We don't deserve and can't do a thing more to deserve, remember? That's the key. Very thought changing.

That is the secret of the Five Star blessings; we don't deserve, but He wants to bless us. We need to accept that, look for it, and know we can't do anything more to deserve it!

I want to add here, to bring this thought home, if we're like most, we may be having a problem still on this word, deserve. There is no balance at times in our Christian culture. The need to serve and deserve can be done in most Christian's lives with no balance, making shame, guilt, and the "we don't deserve" mentality set in. The thoughts that we are not worthy follow right behind deserve. Quite a combination that will go nowhere. All I see there is a "Dead End" sign at the end of that road.

In our Christian culture, it is sometimes about the "I" and not Jesus, if we are not careful. We do all these works, ministries, jobs, and more in hopes to make us feel worthy to deserve. And then the flip side of this coin is just as bad—we feel guilty anytime we do need to put ourselves first and not do all the works on the list, which is the ruler we have for deserving.

If working full time, children, home and life keep us from helping as much as we would like to, then we don't feel worthy to deserve. We are coming and going through a path of guilt. There has to be a healthy balance, and there isn't in this kind of life.

For instance, if someone is full-time in a ministry position—and let's remind ourselves here, that's usually a full-time, paid job—they are doing things for God most of us can't do because of our full-time jobs…I'm saying all this because people who can only volunteer their free time cannot compare what they do or don't do with someone in a paid, full-time position in a church.

In our Christian culture, a lot of people are judging that they are not doing enough to deserve, like a pastor would… I'm not taking away from what a full-time minister is doing, God bless the full-time ministers and missionaries, but that is their job. That is what they are getting paid to do. Again, I'm not taking away from the burden or calling in these positions; however the truth here, using this example, is it wouldn't be smart for a mother of two with a full-time job to compare herself to Joyce Meyer.

> *For by grace, you have been saved through faith, and that not of yourselves; it is the gift of God, not of works, lest anyone should boast. For we are His workmanship, created in Christ Jesus for good works, which God prepared beforehand that we should walk in them.*
> *~ Ephesians 2: 8-10*

I hope we all capture the wisdom in the examples here in this book. In our Christian culture when religion shadows over all the beliefs, myths, and what we've been trained to think about what God wants from us, I pray we get a real relationship with God—no more religion—just a pure, unadulterated relationship with Him. Let Him do with our lives what He wants to do with it.

Ministry is everywhere: at our jobs, in our neighborhood, at the mall, at the bank, the beach…everywhere. I know the fight here. I have lived it and brought the t-shirt souvenirs. As His child, full of love in our heart for Him, we do want to do something! That is our nature as a child of faith. Faith promotes Godly works, but we need to trust Him, that we will do what He has placed in our hearts to do, not because it will make us more worthy to deserve. He knows our heart and wants to bless us, as He blesses the Kingdom.

Ministry - the action of ministering to someone.

We need to be who we are in Christ. Again, works will not get us one more inch "of worthy to deserve." Remember that! "As His child who is walking with Him, we need to trust we will do what's pleasing to Him, and if we need to head in another direction, He will guide us." We need to trust in that and His Five Star blessings. Our ministry blessings are unlimited; He sent us out. Trust Him to do all because He wants to, not that we can make ourselves more deserving. We already have Him, we are His and He is ours.

Reflection Questions –

What comes to your mind concerning the word deserve?

How does God look at the word and us?

Can you receive gifts well?

Has religion clouded your vision of what God has for you?

5
accepting God's love in peace

The previous chapter on the word deserve could have been heavy and thought-provoking for some of us. A few of us may still not be in total agreement on what we just read. We could be in such doubt and trying to figure out if that thought process is Scriptural and could that really be God's way? Could our works really not bring more worth and deserving into our lives? In the Scriptures, we read that we are saved by faith; and our faith will have works, but we aren't saved more by works, so no man could boast on that principal. Makes sense, right? And if the Word of God says it, it is truth, but do we truly walk in the peace of that Scripture? Most of our training in life has said, and trained us to act the exact opposite. If we have been trained that works save us, in time, we can be untrained, and God can give us a new mind and receive His love in peace.

For instance, at the job, if we sell well or bring our company to great heights, we may get a promotion, a bonus, win a great trip, or see a huge pay raise. We usually don't have any problem accepting those bonuses because we worked very hard for them. We've even expected that sort of treatment due to our hard work and think we should be compensated. I would think it is fair to say for the most part, we accept hard work can pay off and should be rewarded.

On the other hand, I think it's fair to say in our culture, we think nothing is for free. Nothing comes easy, and we shouldn't expect anything unless we work for it, right? I'd say we may even agree that expecting too much is detrimental to us, too, due to the fact that dreams sometimes don't happen, life is hard, and well, we need to protect ourselves from all the letdown. Am I right? I would also say most positive people would not want to admit they battle this, too, but at the same time, fight each and every one of these thoughts.

So, how do we get to the place where we accept God's love, blessings, and abundant life in peace? How do we receive the Five Star blessings without all the guilt, thinking we still don't deserve?

Do we think we have to be super spiritual?
Do we mentally have a ruler that we aren't quite measuring up to?

Are we right now picturing a few items in our lives that have to be cleaned up, so this will work in our lives? What we feel on the inside will manifest on the outside. Have we heard messages like we're a failure? Have people spoken falsehoods into our lives? Have we made mistakes? Has our past been crazy and riddled with sin and shame? Have people's belief in our self-worth been hindering? Has our self- esteem been attacked?

Do we not regularly attend a church, or not attend one at all and think we can't be a Christian without a church home? Do we think people who do a lot of Christian-type works are more pure than us? Are we fighting guilt from not reading the bible enough? Guilt for not measuring up? Are we comparing ourselves to others? These few situations are common and can put a person on a downward slope quickly.

Last question: do we think God does not give us things, answer our prayers, or even know our name? Let's take a moment here and try to focus honestly on where exactly we could be.

No matter where we find ourselves, God loves us and truly wants an abundant Five Star life for each of us. We can't limit Him with our limits. So again, we can't do anything to get Him to love us more and we can't do anything to deserve more, but He still wants us to have all He has for us.

> *But God demonstrates His own love toward us, in that while we were still sinners, Christ died for us. ~ Romans 5:8*
> *Trust in the Lord with all your heart, and lean not on your own understanding. In all your ways acknowledge Him, And He shall direct your paths. ~ Proverbs 3:5-6*
>
> *Being confident of this very thing, that He who has begun a good work in you will complete it until the day of Jesus Christ. ~ Philippians 1:6*

Relationships in the natural realm can be difficult and challenging. We have to take time for them. We have to make plans to enjoy them. Good friends can go days, months, and sometimes years without seeing each other and pick right up where they left off. I'm not encouraging us to do that with the Lord, but I hope you get my drift here. Meaning, if we can't mentally remember the last time we picked up the Word of God or said a prayer, which is just talking to God by the way, then the way to pick up where we left off is pick up the Word of God and talk to Him. He is still our friend and our heavenly Father. He may be really missing us. He may be shaking His head at us because we are so lost at times, but He still loves us and is still everything He said He would be to each one of us!

Again, it's relationship. Believe He is there, because He is.

Talk to Him. Picture Him in the passenger seat of your vehicle. Picture Him in the kitchen chair. Picture Him at your side. Just do it; there's no big mystery or master plan to it, just talk to Him and receive. Listen and receive.

I'm not sure in this human form if we ever arrive to a perfect place of never doubting this again. But having this knowledge, we can believe. We can have peace and trust in a God that knows who we are because He created us. We aren't a mistake because He created us; He is the great I AM and with us. So, if the great I AM says trust me, believe in me, I've got this, who are we to argue?

Our peace in this truth can fluctuate like the tide. We can have peace, and then it is gone like our belief that God works like this. We will question our very beliefs, our worthiness of His love, and if He really want to bless us on a Five Star level? This question, even after preaching and affirming our blessings to ourselves, can and will pop back up like an unwanted weed. So, how do we accept that God wants us to have a Five Star blessed life and keep that belief in total accepting peace? I ask that again, because most of us are already doubting it's there for good; we think, at least some of us, that somehow we will goof it up, or God will take it away.

By the end of this book, I hope we all personally grasp God's way better and have a truer understanding of what it really means to be His child. Never measure His love for us by troubles. That is learned behavior we all need to unlearn. He loves us all the time; we will always have troubles and turmoil, and that is where we will see God shine. When something seems impossible for us, but we are waiting on Him and expecting His help—that's where we will see the Five Star life.

Reflection Questions –

Do we have our own mental ruler of measuring up? And if so, does it line up with God?

Has our worth and self-esteem been attacked? If so, in what areas?

Where have you found yourself? Are you limiting or ready to expect God's love in peace?

6

what can hinder our five star life?

This chapter title poses a very good question. What can hinder our Five Star life? After giving this a lot of thought, I believe that the number one hindrance could be we don't know if Five Star life even exists. That it does exist and it will be given to us from our Lord and Savior Jesus Christ—this could be a total shock right now to most minds. Most of us may be thinking, "You mean an abundant life could really exist for me?"

What I mean by not knowing is that we haven't given this way of thinking any thought before. In the past, maybe hints came our way in Sunday school or by our grandmother; but when we got close to even beginning to understand this, we didn't take the time to go deeper into His word, or our imaginations never journeyed in this direction. Maybe it was as simple as we just plain missed it. Any of these descriptions still have the same ending results which is we were hindered and still are.

The number two hindrance could be—after hearing Scriptures in Sunday school, hearing preaching on God's love for us, or any other way we may have received knowledge that God truly wants His best for us—we may have heard it, but it didn't register. This sounded off a blank board in our minds. It may have sounded nice for the moment, but we didn't think on it, we didn't claim it, and/or we didn't let the truth of it touch us. The biggest wall in our minds: it wasn't for us, so why get serious about it? Most of us didn't take the first step of faith to believe after hearing because it couldn't be for us, right? We haven't done enough to deserve it, or we believe the lie that we've never measured up. Or it's always for someone else, especially someone more spiritual, but never for us. We've all been there. What matters now is where we are going with this in the future.

The number three hindrance can be expectations. Are we even looking for something good to happen? Are we even expecting our desires to come true? As we go through our day, have we stopped for a moment and expected something great from God? Days can go by, months can go by, years can go by, and we may never have truly expected something on a Five Star level from above. We may have whined, cried, and prayed a little, but we never expected, in faith, anything fantastic from God. I know it goes back to the "do we deserve feelings?" But let's change that. Remember, there's nothing we can do to deserve more. It's all about Him, and He wants to give a Five Star life for us.

I've looked back over my own past; and I can tell from those memories, I never really focused on anything that would have been considered an expectation in God. I may have been really focused on praying for something, but not really expecting. I'm sure I thought I was walking in complete faith, but wasn't really watching with an expectation. This realization was a huge "wow" to me. I prayed a lot, I talked to God a lot, and I heard Him all the time, but was I actually expecting? I was blessed, and He answered my prayers all the time, but was I expecting Him to answer them? My goodness, was He there for me all the time, despite myself? Well, that was me in the past, and it could be me again. That is why we need to remind ourselves of His love for us and how He wants to give His blessings to us. Remember, it has nothing to do with us; it is all about Him!

It is worth asking again:
Are we really expecting something great?
Are we looking for the Five Star life in God?
Are we praying, but not really expecting?

Faith and expectation are almost the same. Faith is complete trust in something, someone, or God. Expectation is believing something is or will happen. From my perspective, this about sums it up; but at times, the word trust could be iffy if we are being completely honest, right? So, if we have faith in something, let's say God, then by definition we should have complete trust. If I were to guess right, I think most of us say we trust in God. But do we? Completely? When we doubt our deserving, does our trust waiver? Does that "deserving thing" hinder our trust? And then if it does, does our not completely trusting with expectation hinder our expectations and our Five Star living?

Faith – Complete trust or confidence in someone or something.

Expectation – A strong belief that something will happen or be the case in the future.

It's worth thinking about and doing a little soul searching here. Any soul searching we do right now should be written down, so we don't forget. Please grab a notepad and write down any thoughts at this time.

The number four hindrance can be people who have projected their belief system onto us. Are we believing something we've been taught from others, that doesn't line up with what God has for us? One of our biggest influences in life is people. We've heard famous quotes repeated over and over; the people in our lives have been known for projecting certain phrases, and the people we love have personality traits and belief systems that have influenced us since before we could walk.

Our parents, grandparents, friends, teachers, and co-workers have played a huge part in our lives. Their teachings have directed our course, our paths, and sometimes our decisions in every part of our lives. If we've heard a negative belief system and famous quotes that our loved ones are known for saying, but may not be right, we are influenced and maybe not for the good, especially the Five-Star God kind of good.

For example, if we've heard our whole life, the phrase: Money doesn't grow on trees, what did that really say to us? Or this one's good: Don't eat that; it goes straight to the hips. How about this one? Santa's making a list and checking it twice! What do these simple statements say to us? What impression and influence are they making in our minds? Thoughts of not measuring up to some kind of ruler pop into my mind. Or I may not ever have what I want because there is never enough, or enjoy something and you pay in some kind of way. They are not good rulers to measure our lives by, not at all. Those kind of well-known statements throughout the past decades have been put into our minds until we don't even question them anymore…we live by them.

Influences and words are hard to forget. How much time and what will it take for us to forget those negative thoughts that have trained us to think a certain way? These are good questions to ask ourselves and find the answer to. God can reprogram our minds; He can heal our hearts and give us a new thought pattern, which can include the Five Star life He wants us to have.

The declarations into our lives that aren't true and of a good report have to stop. We must not live by false declarations, myths, or fantasy. A Five Star life is real and given to us from above because He says we deserve it. God wants His children to look to Him for all their needs. He wants our expectations to be BIG in him. Again, we can never do anything to deserve more, if the Lord says we deserve a Five Star life, then we deserve a Five Star life through Him. It really takes the pressure off, when we put the focus back on Him, His word, and His promises. We can sit back, believe, and receive.

How do we stop the influencers? The words and memories in our minds can be hard to control, and the negative ones can be difficult to replace with positive ones. If we have the want to, we can do all things through Christ, who strengthens us. It starts with the mind: focusing, lifting ourselves up, and changing our thoughts. This can work with what I like to call positive replacement.

Positive Replacement is replacing all the old, bad, and negative with new, good, and positive. Replace unbelief with belief. Out with the old, negative thoughts and in with the new, positive thoughts.

To encourage our mind—staying in God's word, lifting ourselves up in our most holy faith, and taking back control of what we listen to, watch, and feed our minds with—is a positive plan. We might have to stay away from a negative friend once in a while or change the channel on the TV or even get off social media for a length of time.

Our minds, just like our bodies, can be influenced. What we feed them will influence the health of each. What are we feeding our minds? Who or what are we listening to? Where do we allow random thoughts to take our minds? Are we drifting off the edge of a cliff every few minutes with attacking thoughts sent like fiery darts from the enemy? These are all situations we must recognize and learn to deal with. Spiritual warfare is real, and knowing what we could be dealing with is the first step in helping ourselves combat it.

The Lord has a Five Star plan for each of us. He came to give us life abundantly. This should be a daily reminder and a continued positive reminder throughout the day. Rope yourself back in throughout the day with positive replacement. Develop this habit of bringing your thoughts back under control and the blood of Jesus. This trained warfare will help, and in time become habit so we are no longer led to and fro in our thoughts, but leading a Five Star life in Him.

Five Star God

Reflection Questions –

Have you expected and looked for your blessings on a regular basis?

Do you battle trust? If so, in what areas are your battles?

Will you do positive replacement? How will you go about it?

7

why does God want to bless us?

We get to know God by His word, and from His word we know that God is love, and we are His children. With that alone, without any further research into His word or from any personal experience, we can acknowledge God would want to bless us and is going to bless us on those two things: He is love and we are His children. Now, that being said, most of us, right now, will still have trouble believing He wants to bless us.

For most of us, our belief system is based on something we saw or felt personally. To believe means to accept something as true, feel something is true, have faith, hold something as a strong opinion or suppose. It's hard for some of us to believe without seeing, so how can we believe God wants to love and bless us when we haven't been loved and blessed by others we can see and feel? Having a belief system in a God who wants to love us is not an easy road for those who have been hurt, not shown love, and not blessed by the ones whom they love. But with God all things are possible!

Five Star God

But Jesus looked at them and said to them, "With men this is impossible, but with God all things are possible." ~ Matthew 19:26

When we believe in something, a lot of the time, we haven't seen the end result of what we are believing in. Our belief is mixed with a whole lot of faith. Our faith helps us believe. Our belief helps us have faith. When we strongly believe in something we have never seen, and we hold strong that what we believe in is going to happen and/or we accept something we've never seen, that's belief. We can believe. It's possible all the time.

A faith in God is just like the previous paragraph, we have not seen God, face to face, but we can believe in Him. We have not seen the healing yet, but we can believe in it. We don't have the job yet, but we can believe and feel the job is coming. We haven't felt God in days, weeks, and maybe years, but we believe He's still there. We don't see Him, but we can still believe we feel Him near. A faith in His Five Star blessings is the same; we know He wants it for us because He loves us, and we are His creation, His child. A loving Father wants the best for His children.

The following scriptures are some of my favorites because they remind us He is here to bless us with His Five Star blessings.

He is with us and He is our God!
Fear not, for I am with you; be not dismayed, for I am your God; I will strengthen you, I will help you, I will uphold you with my righteous right hand. ~ Isaiah 41:10

We don't have to lean on our own understanding!
We can trust Him! Trust in the Lord with all your heart, and do not lean on your own understanding. ~ Proverbs 3:5

He gives us our future and hope!
For I know the plans I have for you, declares the Lord, plans for welfare and not for evil, to give you a future and a hope. ~ Jeremiah 29:11

He will command blessings in all we do!
The Lord will command the blessing on you in your barns and in all that you undertake. And He will bless you in the land that the Lord your God is giving. ~ Deuteronomy 28:8

He is our husband, our redeemer, and takes care of us!
For your Maker is your husband, the Lord of hosts is His name; and the Holy One of Israel is your Redeemer, the God of the whole earth He is called. ~ Isaiah 54:5

He is good to all!
The Lord is good to all, and His mercy is over all that He has made. ~ Psalms 145:9

He is compassionate to us!
As a father shows compassion to his children, so the Lord shows compassion to those who fear Him. ~ Psalms 103:13

He has a steadfast love for us, His children!
But the steadfast love of the Lord is from everlasting to everlasting on those who fear Him, and His righteousness to children's children. ~ Psalms 103:17

He loves us with an everlasting love!
The Lord appeared to Him from far away. I have loved you with an everlasting love; therefore, I have continued my faithfulness to you. ~ Jeremiah 31:3

He gives us power to get wealth; He takes care of us!
You shall remember the Lord your God, for it is He who gives you power to get wealth that He may confirm His covenant that He swore to your fathers, as it is this day. ~ Deuteronomy 8:18

He is in us and has overcome!
Little children, you are from God and have overcome them, for He who is in you is greater than He who is in the world. ~ I John 4:4

His face shines upon us and gives us peace!
The Lord bless you and keep you; the Lord make His face to shine upon you and be gracious to you; the Lord lift up His countenance upon you and give you peace. ~ Numbers 6:24-26

He will meet all our needs!
And my God will meet all your needs according to the riches of His glory in Christ Jesus. ~ Philippians 4:19

He does not change and every good gift is from above!
Every good and perfect gift is from above, coming down from the Father of the heavenly lights, who does not change like shifting shadows. ~ James 1:17

He will uphold us; we are not to fear, and He will help us!
So do not fear, for I am with you; do not be dismayed, for I am your God. I will strengthen you and help you; I will uphold you with my righteous right hand. ~ Isaiah 41:10

He rejoices over us and will quiet us by His love!
The Lord your God is in your midst, a mighty one who will save; He will rejoice over you with gladness; He will quiet you by his love; He will exult over you with loud singing. ~ Zephaniah 3:17

Though we walk through trouble, He preserves and saves us!
Though I walk in the midst of trouble, you preserve my life. You stretch out your hand against the anger of my foes; with your right hand you save me. ~ Psalm 138:7

He is our refuge; we shall not fear!
The Lord is on my side; I will not fear. What can man do to me? The Lord is on my side as my helper; I shall look in triumph on those who hate me. It is better to take refuge in the Lord, than to

> *trust in man. It is better to take refuge in the Lord, than to trust in princes. ~ Psalm 118:6-9*

There are many more scriptures on this subject. Study and meditate on these and keep reading the word, because we will find many more that can become our daily reminders. As we get out of bed, one of our daily reminders in the morning should be God is Love and He loves us, His children. What a mighty God we can get to know and serve! What a mighty God we need to get to know better, so we can seek and see His Five Star blessings in our lives.

Again, let's be reminded, our God is a Five Star blessing God, and we can't do anything more to deserve His love or His blessings. We don't deserve, God doesn't want us "doing" to deserve, and He blesses us because of Him. It's always Him; it's always about Him and through Him. It has never been works, and it will never be about works and us earning or deserving His love.

> *For by grace you have been saved through faith, and that not of yourselves; it is the gift of God, not of works, lest anyone should boast. ~ Ephesians 2:8-9*

The most wonderful part of knowing a God like this is it takes all the pressure off of us. It's all about God. Everything is about Him. When we realize it's all God and think on those thoughts when diving into any situation, it will make a huge difference in our daily lives. Every situation or challenge can be looked at this way. Whew, it's not us. When we put Him in the mix, it's about Him!

I realized this wisdom years ago, but being human, we will have to remind ourselves daily. When I'm giving an author talk, as I walk into the room or step up to the podium, I go with God. All pressure comes off when I know He is doing this through me—when it's not about me, but it's about how He can shine through me. I may be nervous for a minute; but once I start speaking what He gave me, all pressure is gone and His peace comes. When I write a book, all pressure is off because I write what God tells me to write because it is His book and His story. When I paint, I paint with what talent God gave me. All pressure is off of me when I know I'm doing my best with what God has given me. It's all Him through me. The confidence we can achieve knowing that it is all God can be mighty useful to us going forward.

Think for a moment what we really could be like and get done in our life knowing God will work through us, God will bless us, and God wants us to succeed. It really would be mind-blowing if we could get ahold of this. Think on the stress, loneliness, and fear we have when we are trying to do everything on our own. We don't get things done well when we are walking in stress, loneliness, and fear, would you think? So, grabbing ahold and focusing on "God's got this" in everything we do could release a lot of this stressful pressure, don't you think? I could list so many benefits here that would be life changing, but just to touch on a few, our health, our relationships, our prosperity, and most of all, our relationship with God.

Reflection Questions –

What is our belief system based on?

How should we start our day?

How can we take the pressure off of us?

8

how do I find the five star God?

We've read in the first chapter what Five Star means in our consumer world. In the last few chapters we have read that a Five Star God exists and that He loves us, His children. We've looked at the word deserve, and how God doesn't measure His love to us by what we deserve, but what He wants to do—and that is love us. The wisdom in this book tells us it's not works, and it's not getting to a place of deserving God's love and blessings; but it's that God wants to love us and God wants to bless us. And He wants to bless us with not a morsel, but a meal; not dangling something before us, but the giving of gifts; not just a life, but an abundant life.

So, if this God exists and we are His children, how do we see Him? That is a good question that needs an answer. Especially to those who have not found Him yet, and to those who have met Him, but may not know where He is now. Let's go over finding Him for good. My hope by the end of this book is we find Him and never let Him go. We develop a relationship with Him, so that even if one of us is quiet, we pick right up where we left off, and everything in our lives is no longer morsels along the way, but daily meals with Him.

If we haven't found God yet, the good news is He's searching for us. He's looking for us to see and find Him. If we've found Him, but we lost track of Him for long periods of time, He's never left us. He's waiting for us to seek Him out again. He's always with us. And if we're walking with Him daily, He's looking for us to get to know Him more and more deeply.

> *And he said to him, "You shall love the Lord your God with all your heart and with all your soul and with all your mind. This is the great and first commandment. And a second is like it: You shall love your neighbor as yourself. On these two commandments depend all the Law and the Prophets. ~ Matthew 22:37-40*

> *And you shall love the Lord your God with all your heart and with all your soul and with all your mind and with all your strength. ~ Mark 12:30*

> *Hear, O Israel: The Lord our God, the Lord is one. You shall love the Lord your God with all your heart and with*

all your soul and with all your might. And these words that I command you today shall be on your heart. You shall teach them diligently to your children, and shall talk of them when you sit in your house, and when you walk by the way, and when you lie down, and when you rise. You shall bind them as a sign on your hand, and they shall be as frontlets between your eyes. ~ Deuteronomy 6:4-9

Let not your hearts be troubled. Believe in God; believe also in me. ~ John 14:1

Rejoice always, pray without ceasing, give thanks in all circumstances; for this is the will of God in Christ Jesus for you. ~ I Thess. 5:16-18

There's so much on the subject of finding God and seeking God, but let's stick with the basics and make this simple, even though sometimes nothing seems simple. We should always be growing, changing, and developing into the person we want to be, as should our relationship with people and God have the same goals. To stay the same would be stagnant, so growing together and maturing together is a natural process that most forget to tend to.

I can only tell you what I know from the Word and my own experience with God. I do know we can continually grow as a person with God. We will always learn something new, and having a relationship with God will never be boring. We think we know it all, and then He shows us something new. We will never know it all, and that is what keeps this relationship quite exciting.

What we can personally come to experience with finding God and knowing He is with us in all things is encountering the believing in His presence. And by that I mean believing He is always with us and He is here with us no matter what the circumstances are, that we're not alone and with childlike behavior always picturing Him with us, sitting right next to us.

I will admit there is a quality to this that we have to stir up, a childlike faith, so to speak. Always believing in something we can't see can be easy some days and practically feel impossible other days. So, don't be hard on yourself if you haven't quite accomplished this yet.

This seems to work when our faith is mixed with believing on a daily basis. Daily because we need to touch God daily: a daily conversation here, some worship and more conversation over there. That way, He can talk to us every day and check in with us to see how we are. When we forget to take God on our daily trips, it feels like He's not there. But reminding ourselves of His presence is the step to feel Him with us.

A Five Star note here: God is always with us. It's not in

feeling and emotions. He may be quiet or we may have forgotten to take Him along, but rest assured, He's always there. Also, if we don't feel Him, just believe. Eventually, we will know He's there because He is.

When we talk to someone, we get to know him by listening to the tone of his voice and his language. By language, I'm referring to how people express themselves, how they describe things, and how their outlook on things comes through their voice and body language. We will not clearly understand what someone is saying to us if we don't know them. When we get to know someone, the understanding comes when they interact with us. They could say something that could confuse one person, but we totally get what they are saying because we know them.

When we get to know God's voice, we will have a better understanding of who He is and what exactly He is saying to us. Talking with Him and taking Him with us through our daily activities will put us in His presence. To be in God's presence is where we want to be.

We will have rest!
And He said, "My presence will go with you, and I will give you rest." ~ Exodus 33:14

We will have joy and pleasures forevermore!
You make known to me the path of life; in your presence, there

*is fullness of joy; at your right hand are pleasures forevermore.
~ Psalm 16:11*

We will find Him!
You will seek me and find me, when you seek me with all your heart. ~ Jeremiah 29:13

We will see His beauty and be able to refresh ourselves!
*One thing have I asked of the Lord, that will I seek after: that I may dwell in the house of the Lord all the days of my life, to gaze upon the beauty of the Lord and to inquire in his temple.
~ Psalm 27:4*

He protects us in His presence!
Oh, how abundant is your goodness, which you have stored up for those who fear you and worked for those who take refuge in you, in the sight of the children of mankind! In the cover of your presence you hide them from the plots of men; you store them in your shelter from the strife of tongues. ~ Psalm 31:19-20

We can abide in Him and Him in us!
So we have come to know and to believe the love that God has for us. God is love, and whoever abides in love abides in God, and God abides in him. ~ I John 4:16

Each of us is uniquely different and so are our relationships and approaches to God. Entering His presence will vary, but the way is the same. Talk with God, worship Him, and seek Him out daily. No rules, no pretense, just seek out a pure friendship and develop a personal relationship with Him. I do believe we make it harder than it is due to walls in our lives, fears, and just simply not knowing the truth about our God.

While you're driving, picture Him in the passenger seat and start talking. When we're fearful, take a hold of His hand. Literally reach across and take hold of it. I did that over a month of everyday radiation treatments. Believe me, it works! Are you feeling anxiety? Call upon Him.

But more important than calling on Him just when we truly need Him, we need to get into His presence and just get to know Him. Let Him be in us and us in Him.

Think about that for a minute: the Lord God All Mighty is in us. And us in Him. When we become one with Him, He's in us and we're in Him. I can still picture myself at an author speaking engagement at a college in Grand Rapids, Michigan. This talk was scheduled after I received this wisdom: it's all God and not us. I had just started my journey trying to live it. I was a nervous wreck when I arrived at the college. Upon walking in, I was taking deep breaths trying to calm myself. When I arrived, everyone was so excited and happy to see me, and I think that made me even more nervous. Their high expectations were so clear in their eyes, and that scared me so much more.

Honestly, I'm a behind-the-scenes type of person, being in the forefront is not easy for me.

When I walked into the room, it was packed. I smiled through the fear and walked up to the podium, taking my notes and books out of my satchel. My hands were shaking. "Oh, great" is what I thought. Nerves and all. Then all of the sudden, my mind cleared and my thought was I was not alone, and I should just let God take over. I have to tell you what I did. I mentally stepped aside, and called upon God and let Him go for it. I looked up at the room full of students and teachers and said to myself, "Okay, Jesus, let's see what you can do." I had a peace come over me and started talking. The only remnant of my nerves showed in the last shiver of my hands while I gathered up my papers. It was amazing—the kindness, the wisdom, and the direction for these students that came out of me. It was all God.

I had their attention, and they were dreaming big, writing notes and fully active with me in their body language. It was an amazing hour and a half. After the author chat, they treated me like I was something special. I knew what they were drawn to was God because He talked to them that morning. He inspired their dreams, and He gave them direction. Through me, maybe, but it was all Him. And now knowing that took a thousand pounds of pressure off of me.

I shared the above example to show what I experienced when walking in the faith of knowing God was with me, in me, and would work through me. Do I have that faith in the first moments of every trying situation in my life? No, I don't. Our humanness will always be there; but what I love about believing is our faith that our Five Star God can always be there, too.

Reflection Questions –

Have your found God or is He searching for you?

How can we find God?

When we know He's with us, how can that change our lives?

9

will God be a five star God to me?

Will God do for us what we're learning in this book? Will He be a Five Star God to us? To each of us, we ask? After reading these past chapters, most of us are still pondering this question in the back of our minds. While reading this book, we may have already thought of several people we think, "God has blessed them, but He's never blessed me like that." Right? Well, again, I'm glad to write these words...you are not alone.

We've all been there; we see people with a relationship with God that many could envy. We see people getting married, getting a good job, or buying a new house; or they are so healthy and active that we feel sick instead of happy for them. And to top it off, all we've done the past few years is gain weight or had to change jobs, and buying a house is totally out of our financial range. Sound familiar? Or maybe just a little bit? Again, you're not alone.

Whether we are battling these thoughts right now or not, we can get those kinds of thoughts plopping themselves into our minds, causing a boat load of fun getting over them. The fight is never fun getting on track in our faith and beliefs, nor is it fun being confused about God's love, even for a moment. The battlefield of our souls is between our ears; and if the enemy of our souls can make us miserable and lonely, he knows we will focus on that junk for a while and forget the most important thing is God loves us and will take care of us.

God's Word say He loved us before we loved Him. He knew us before the womb, and He sent His Son because of His love for us. God doesn't have favorites, even though we'd all like to think so at times. We use that as a defense to justify what we don't understand and the lack of seeing anything happening in our lives. Human nature is to blame and then we act as if we didn't care anyway.

He loves each of us and wants an abundant life for all of us. Since He's a Five Star God, He can and will be a Five Star God to each of us. He does this and wants this because He does. Period. It's His word.

He shows us His love while we are yet sinners. He draws us by His love. He blesses us, so we may see Him. We all have a Five Star God who loves us! If, when, and where may be a problem...It is us knowing, seeing, asking, and accepting this from Him. Again, we don't have to do works and more to deserve; we just need to believe this knowledge by knowing, wait for it by seeing, or even better, by looking for it. We need to talk to Him by asking, and we need to open our hearts and tear down the walls to accept. No questions asked, just accept and let thankfulness shine and glorify Him.

There's so little on our part. The "little" is not always easy sometimes because we have to trust in Him. We may have to wait for it to be worked out. Waiting can be made easier by being open to something better and looking for the bigger picture. We can get focused on one little tidbit and miss the whole thing being done around us. Things are not always as they appear. We must remember this when taking control of our thoughts.

While still a sinner, God died for us!
While still a sinner, He loved us and died for us. But God shows His love for us in that while we were still sinners, Christ died for us. ~ Romans 5:8

We can find God!
I love those who love me, and those who seek me diligently find me. ~ Proverbs 8:17

We can be accepted by God, no partiality!
So Peter opened his mouth and said: "Truly I understand that

Five Star God

God shows no partiality, but in every nation, anyone who fears Him and does what is right is acceptable to Him. ~ Acts 10:34-35

God loves us; He sent His son!
This is love, not that we have loved God but that He loved us and sent his Son to be the propitiation for our sins. ~ I John 4:10

He fulfills His promise!
The Lord is not slow to fulfill his promise as some count slowness, but is patient toward you, not wishing that any should perish, but that all should reach repentance. ~ II Peter 3:9

He wants us to have a future and hope!
For I know the plans I have for you, declares the Lord, plans for welfare and not for evil, to give you a future and a hope. ~ Jeremiah 29:11

He will strengthen and help us!
Fear not, for I am with you; be not dismayed, for I am your God; I will strengthen you, I will help you, I will uphold you with my righteous right hand. ~ Isaiah 41:10

Nothing can separate us from the love of God!
Who shall separate us from the love of Christ? Shall tribulation, or distress, or persecution, or famine, or nakedness, or danger, or sword? As it is written, "For your sake, we are being killed all the day long; we are regarded as sheep to be slaughtered." No, in all

these things, we are more than conquerors through Him who loved us. For I am sure that neither death nor life, nor angels nor rulers, nor things present nor things to come, nor powers, nor height nor depth, nor anything else in all creation, will be able to separate us from the love of God in Christ Jesus our Lord. ~ Romans 8:35-39

He heals the brokenhearted!
He heals the brokenhearted and binds up their wounds. ~ Psalms 147:3

He abides in us, and we abide in Him!
So we have come to know and to believe the love that God has for us. God is love, and whoever abides in love abides in God, and God abides in him. ~ I John 4:16

He continues His faithfulness to us!
The Lord appeared to him from far away. I have loved you with an everlasting love; therefore I have continued my faithfulness to you. ~ Jeremiah 31:3

He first loved us!
We love because He first loved us. ~ I John 4:19

He is the door!
I am the door. If anyone enters by me, he will be saved and will go in and out and find pasture. The thief comes only to steal and kill and destroy. I came that they may have life and have it abundantly. I am the good shepherd. The good shepherd lays

down his life for the sheep. ~ John 10:9-11

His mercy never ends!
The steadfast love of the Lord never ceases; His mercies never come to an end; they are new every morning; great is your faithfulness. ~ Lamentations 3:22-23

He will rejoice over us!
The Lord your God is with you, the Mighty Warrior who saves. He will take great delight in you; in his love he will no longer rebuke you, but will rejoice over you with singing. ~ Zephaniah 3:17

The part of God we all have access to is His word and by reading His word, we can see He has done a lot for us already. Before we were born, He already died for us. He had a plan from the beginning for those who love Him. He's the perfect father who will always take care of His children because He's a Five Star God.

I know from personal experience that after reading this last paragraph, and reading the previous chapters, some of us just experienced a moment of doubt or unbelief. There is still something inside causing us to cringe or speculate a little. I do believe believing in something we cannot see, nor do we know is a sure thing, is not necessarily an easy thing to do. When all we have to do is believe, it can be the hardest thing to accomplish. We can still doubt the truth even though we know the truth. We can think He won't love us the way He loves others even though the facts, His love and His word, say differently. We can still battle a battle that has already been won.

My own personal experience has shown me that I move back or I get uncomfortable when love is shown me. It's involuntary, but I sense it. So, do we pull back or cringe even slightly when faced with God's love? Do we find it so hard to believe that we don't accept it? Believe me, He loves us. He loves us so much He came and died, so we didn't have to.

Every day, pushing away the doubt and opening the door of our hearts for His love will allow Him to be a Five Star God to each of us. Replacing all unbelief with a spoken word of worship to Him. Even if we don't truly believe anything yet, we need to do this in faith of something good to come. Old habits need to be replaced; old ways need to be forgotten; old ways of thinking need to be fixed and repaired with new thoughts.

When our old habits are replaced with His Five Star God ways, we will be amazed at what it will change in our everyday life. Seeing a future in faith that could be ours is life changing. Having something to believe in saves our future. Knowing God is with us and has our backs are game changers. Being a friend of God is the best relationship we could ever cultivate!

Five Star God

So, can God be a Five Star to us? Yes, He can and already is! I get so excited about what He's going to do for me; I can jump up and down on what I know He's going to do for YOU!

Reflection Questions –

Are we alone? How have we felt alone?

Is believing an easy thing to do? What hinders us?

What habits do we have that can hinder us from a Five Star belief?

10

who can keep us from our five star God?

No one can separate us from our Five Star God, but can we be kept from Him? Can we be hindered in our doubt and unbelief? Can people or situations keep us from God and a relationship with Him? I don't believe anything can keep us from Him, anything...but I do believe we can let situations and people in our lives keep us from Him without even knowing we are doing so.

For instance:

1. Lies – We can believe lies about God, who He is, and not knowing His Word for ourselves; we can even believe lies about His Word—lies we've been told since we were a child, lies about ourselves and our self-worth, or lies from people that have been jealous or agenda seeking. The biggest lies that come daily—lies from the enemy of our souls. The enemy of our souls knows if he can be subtle and twist the word just a bit with his lies, he can keep us busy trying to figure things out. A lie is a lie and will never be the truth. The devil is the father of lies and always will be.

2. People – I see this mostly with people we love or people in an authority position. The people we love may not want God in their lives, so they try to hinder us having Him in ours. Some people can feel so threatened; they do everything in their power to stop us from seeking God. A spouse who is not with God may absolutely hate us having a relationship with Him. A boss at work may pick up on who we are with God and put the brakes on promoting us. Parents who are not close with God may not want their child anywhere near Him. It may not be obvious either; the enemy of our souls could use people to hurt us, say awful things about us, and accuse us of wrongful doings that we had no part in; however we may blame God not seeing His help in any of it, which in return hinders our relationships due to the lies believed.

3. Health – Our health problems could be making us at an all-time low that we can't feel God; we are only feeling pain. Illness will weaken the body, which will cause havoc in our minds. When we are trying to heal and get our strength back, it can be almost impossible to find God's hand and hang on. God has not left us, even though it may feel it at times to the weakened state of the body. He will pick us up and put us in the water when it is stirring. He has not left us. Chronic pain and diseases that are incurable can cause so much pain and fear we can be consumed. Death can't separate us from God, but facing it could be very scary and fearful. We are human, not perfect, human...being scared and feeling alone in situations is normal. We do have God on our side to help us through everything, and that is what we have to take hold of and not let go!

4. Ourselves – Us? We could be the one keeping us from God? Yes. The answer here could be anything and of any angle because we are so unique. It could be personality, past hurts, past belief system, our own lusts, no trust, sins, past sins, life, no depth, ignorance, stubbornness, limits, health limits, fears, anger, sadness, loss, blind understanding, no understanding, no faith, crushed faith, accusations, lazy, doubt, unbelief, deceived, believing our own excuses, and lies. Yes, we can hinder ourselves.

5. Outside circumstances beyond our control – These type of circumstances happen, and we may not know why, nor do we know why we feel far from God during them. These are the awful, God only knows situations, with people, jobs, weather, health, or anything else that just seems like all we can say is, "What?" We keep keeping on; we move forward with God and chalk it up to: we have no idea what in the world this is. And when God wants us to know, let's pray He lets us know, but only if we need to know. Trust me, we don't want to know until He knows we can handle it. Does weird stuff happen? Yes, it does. Do we or can we always know why? I think some things are just better left alone and trust God. Easy? No. But He has our best interest at heart. Remember He's a Five Star God and nothing less.

> *Who shall separate us from the love of Christ? Shall tribulation, or distress, or persecution, or famine, or nakedness, or danger, or sword? As it is written, "For your sake, we are being killed all the day long; we are regarded as sheep to be slaughtered." No, in all these things, we are more than conquerors through Him who loved us. For I am sure that neither death nor life, nor angels nor rulers, nor things present nor things to come, nor powers, nor height nor depth, nor anything else in all creation will be able to separate us from the love of God in Christ Jesus our Lord.*
> *~ Romans 8:35-39*

> *Put on the whole armor of God that you may be able to stand against the schemes of the devil.*
> *~ Ephesians 6:11*

Nothing can separate us from Jesus. God loved us so much He robed himself in flesh and walked among us. Then He died for us. Then He rose again on the third day and stayed among those that loved Him, teaching them, so they could teach us, and we can teach others. Then He rose to His place in heaven and sent his Spirit back on the day of Pentecost, so we truly didn't have to feel left alone. He's with us and in us, and we are in Him. Having a relationship with Him that really means something makes it real, honest, picks right up every time where it left off, and you're never really separated; you're always together!

I'd like to elaborate on number four from above. When dealing with ourselves, I saw something about myself that I mentioned in an earlier chapter. When given gifts for no apparent reason or earning, I had a very hard time accepting them. I searched my heart for the why. Why was this hard for me? When I asked wisdom from above, this is the wisdom God showed me, and it all had to do with personality, training, and I do believe, religion. The word deserve is what God showed me, and then He showed me the true meaning of the word when God looks upon us.

My why was I didn't feel like I deserved. I had to think on this—the gifts and kindness made me feel uncomfortable. I wasn't walking around in guilt and shame, but gifts, kindness, and love were putting me on the spot. It bought out a defense against intimacy, and that can be the fear of getting hurt. Being vulnerable is not easy; it makes you feel you're losing control. We really don't have control over anything, so I don't know why we fight for it so much.

To think I deserved made me feel bad from the years of hearing: "It's better to give than to receive." There's always someone who could need it more than me, and I could never enjoy the gifts from those inner feelings, so why even get them? Peoples' motives for their gifts and feeling safe are also factors for a lot of people. I think we also have a problem to receive because we couldn't, or we feel the need to impart equally back to them.

The most important key to this book, if we get nothing else, is we don't deserve; we can't do anything to deserve more, and God doesn't want us trying to deserve. He loves us and takes care of us because He wants to. It has nothing to do with us doing something to deserve more.

When I apply this wisdom to my life, it's like the mountains move. When we know God is with us and more than able to open the doors that need to be opened and close the doors that need to be closed, it's amazing what can happen. When we apply and acknowledge His promises in our lives, the best gets better. The spiritual wisdom gets better. Everything gets better because we can have the peace that when we love the Lord, and remember He already more than loves us, we are in Him and He is in us; we are with Him and He is with us; all will work out in the end for His children; He will never leave us or forsake us.

Look for His Five Star blessings—they are everywhere. They can be from the littlest to the biggest. A parking place can open up just in the nick of time; a check comes in the mail when we financially need it; or we get the miracle we've prayed for. The Five Star life with God comes in many ways, unique to us and perfect in every way for our good.

Ginae Lee Scott

Let me tell you a fun Five Star blessing that happened to us when on vacation. We booked a hotel room that was in the range of what we could pay for. When we got there, I have to admit I was somewhat disappointed because we had no view from our balcony as it was mostly the parking lot below. All of us were kind of bummed, but I wasn't going to complain to my husband and was trying to be positive about it. I kept pointing out the good things, like when we leaned way out from the balcony, we could see the beach. We left the room to go explore and get something to eat. When we left, we noticed the bathroom had some water on the floor around the toilet so we let the front desk know before we left for dinner, just in case something was really wrong.

We had a great evening and when we came back, the front desk sent up a man right away to take our luggage to another room because the water from the toilet was leaking, and they didn't want their guests hassling with it. We told them it was no big deal, and they could fix it in the morning, but they wouldn't take no for an answer and insisted we changed rooms. So, we packed up all the items we had already unpacked and followed the hotel staff and the luggage carrier down the hallway. As he went around the corner, the room we were getting was in the middle of an outside balcony and looked over the parking lot. When he opened the door, we were astonished, shocked, and amazed.

We were moved to a suite with full ocean view and a view of the pool and beach below. We were given this room for the entire week, complete with a wonderful living room, kitchen, separate bedrooms, two full bathrooms, and two balconies to enjoy, all compliments of the hotel. We got our room upgraded to a suite, due to a little water on the bathroom floor of the room that was supposed to be ours. I personally saw the Lord all over it. We never even asked for anything from the hotel or God, but God provided for us. This upgrade made our vacation an upgraded vacation!

When we need an answer to something important and we look to Him, we get direction with a bright light on the path. When we need a doctor, He can lead us to the best there is. A job change, which we think would be bad, could be the exact place we need to be for our future. When we have our sights on buying a house and the deal falls through, we could be so discouraged, but it could be an open door for us to get the house He intends for us. How we are looking at situations can also make the situation.

Again, looking for situations that may be directing our paths to a much better Five Star blessing from God is essential. We can't get what we're not looking for or expecting. If we aren't looking for the good, we won't see it. The negative will radiate through. Stop, and take that moment in every situation to really look at what may be going on before going off angry or having some kind of a meltdown.

I'm using situations in the above paragraphs that each of us can relate to, but there are Five Star God situations that can be happening that are not part of the subject of our natural welfare, but our spiritual welfare. God wants to take care of all our natural needs, like food, clothes, housing, transportation, the perfect building for our business, or the right college for our future; but even more is our spiritual welfare for our future with Him. Looking for the spiritual growth He liked to do for us is important also. Are we growing in our Christian character? Do we have needs there that God needs to help us with and are guiding us in certain directions that will be better for us?

Closed doors are not necessarily bad. When one closes, always look for the one that is opening. It's a daily reminder of who we are in Him, who He is in us, and when we are His child--where we stand in our inheritance. Open doors are part of our inheritance in Him!

Think about this for a moment. If there is someone who wants to take care of us, our spiritual needs and our natural needs, who are we to argue? Now, if we are the type of person who thinks we don't need anyone to help us or we don't want any help, then we have a small problem here because we have a God who wants to help us and takes care of us. Having an attitude that communicates "the don't help me" or the "don't give me anything" attitude will get us nowhere.

Five Star God

Reflection Questions –

How do we relate to what can keep us from our Five Star God?

Should we give up at closed doors or look at what God may be doing?

How can we go about looking for what God is doing to better our life?

11

it's day by day

From a previous chapter, I stated how this wonderful notion of God wanting to give to us better and bigger than we can imagine started with the gift of expensive cosmetics from a stranger who said it wasn't his problem I didn't receive gifts well. But, he was giving me the gift.

I'd like to take this opportunity to tell you the next thing that happened, and I felt God sent a stranger again. The next year, my husband and I were given a free trip to the most wonderful island I've ever been on, and we stayed in the most beautiful Five Star hotel. The hotel was the Four Seasons on the island of Anguilla. Honestly, I had never heard of the island before this trip. We were given a week there with all expenses paid; this was a real gift in every sense of the word.

I truly, without stretching any truth, believe that trip was a once in a lifetime trip. From how it worked out that we were given the trip to the destination to our hotel and who

Five Star God

we met on the trip. We met lifelong friends, had memorable experiences, and were taken care of in a Five Star way that we couldn't have even imagined. Spa packages, food, and our room were above and beyond anyone's. How did that happen? I have no idea. Why did it happen? I one hundred percent believe it happened, so God could show me what He was talking about in another example. He can open doors for us that weren't even there. He can make a few small moves in a situation and make it better for us.

Our room had its own small pool on the balcony. It overlooked the beautiful hotel pools, and the ocean just beyond with full views was definitely a room wanted by the rich and famous. We met people at the hotel who booked their trip, booking a room like ours months before, and they told us their trip had required lots of planning and expenses that went into it. They couldn't believe we had won the trip. What I'm saying here is if I had booked a room myself, it would probably have been down the road at another hotel a lot less expensive. If I had done any of this myself with my limitations, it would have been for a lot less in everything.

Now, I'm not telling this story to say God is going to give everyone a trip like this or change our hotel rooms every time we aren't happy with the one we can afford; but what He did use it for, in my little brain, was to show me that He does want a Five Star life for us—blessing us better than we could ever imagine in all things. And He knew I'd write about it because He told me to.

Even after the man who gave me the gift in Vegas, even after the trip to Anguilla, it's still hard to believe that God will take care of us every day and that it isn't going to "cost us." Should it be so hard to believe this after He has proven to us time and time again? Probably not, but as the humans we are, is it easy? No, it's not—not with doubt fighting our minds and the enemy fighting for our soul.

But who knows this more than ourselves? Jesus knows, and He has given us some advice to help us fight in our day to day!

The thief comes only to steal and kill and destroy. I came that they may have life and have it abundantly. ~ John 10:10

In all these things, we are more than conquerors through Him who loved us. ~ Rom. 8:37

Submit yourselves to God. Resist the devil, and he will flee from you. ~ James 4:7

Be self-controlled and alert. Your enemy the devil prowls around like a roaring lion looking for someone to devour. Resist him, standing firm in the faith. ~ 1 Pet. 5:8-9

You are from God, little children, and have overcome them; because greater is He who is in you than he who is in the world. ~ 1 John 4:4

The Lord will cause your enemies who rise against you to be defeated before you. They shall come out against you one way and flee before you seven ways. ~ Deut. 28:7

You will make known to me the path of life; In Your presence is fullness of joy; In Your right hand, there are pleasures forever. ~ Ps. 16:11

There is no fear in love, but perfect love casts out fear. For fear has to do with punishment, and whoever fears has not been perfected in love. We love because He first loved us. ~ 1 Jo. 4:18-19

I believe the unusual gift examples in my life were used to get my attention. I needed to get over my own hindrances to receiving from God. When we can't grasp an understanding why someone would want to just give these things to us, and if we can't grasp that why, then how do we grasp God's why?

When I was on the beach in Anguilla, a woman came up to my husband and I right at the moment I was telling him everything that God was showing me the past months for this book. She came right up to me and stated that I loved Jesus. She didn't ask me; she declared it was true. I nodded my head in the only reply I felt was necessary. And then she proceeded to tell me that God's math didn't add up like our math; a day is a thousand years; a thousand years is a day. She went on and talked about the fishes and loaves of bread that multiplied to feed thousands.

She was driving home to me that our math calculations or expectations don't add up with God. We can't figure it out. We are just to be with Him on this great ride called life, listen to His voice, obey what He's telling us, and not worry when it doesn't add up because with God, it would never add up right to us. We don't do math like God does, and that is for sure!

It was on that beach that day we felt the first nudges of making a move in our lives. If God's equations weren't ours, and with no such limitations, what were we thinking in our heart of hearts? What had we been afraid to do or try? Long story short, we wanted to move somewhere warm. We were very established in West Michigan, our children, our home, and my favorite place, our summer home on a lake. So, what did we do? We started making plans to move, and everything worked out from a new job, home, and the sale of everything we owned in Michigan. It was a wow couple of months with wow Five Star blessings. Looking for God in your life and finding Him involved in everything brings a peace that surpasses all understanding, and that is how He wants us to have life abundant.

When we started to fret at the huge move before us, it was as clear as the day the Five Star was born, along with the wisdom to just take it one day at a time and He will take care of everything.

Five Star God

When I grabbed hold of the Five Star thinking, instead of "the room with no view is all we deserve on vacation" mentality, when I let go of the reins and let Him, and when I obeyed His voice on taking it one day at a time, it was absolutely amazing. We were at our new home right on schedule to the day with the semi-truck loaded down with our belongings pulling up ten minutes after us. His leading and guidance didn't stop there. From Five Star wisdom leading me to a new business idea, leading and using me to write a new book, spiritual wisdom, health help after an awful fall, new friends, and guidance after guidance in a new city where we knew no one, the list goes on and on.

My computer probably couldn't hold the chapters if I listed each Five Star situation that I believe God had His hand in. I don't even remember all that I know God took care of; I wish I could, but my humanness takes over and I forget.

God passes my expectations every day. God surprises me every day. I do have bigger ideas because of His encouragement, and He still surprises me. Is life perfect? Life will never be perfect except moments here and there. But can it be amazing and be filled with wonderful Five Star surprises? Yes! And we should look for them everywhere and every day! Has my life been perfect? No, life for me was a little crazy after our move, but wonderful at the same time if that makes any sense. Wonderful because through it all, I knew He was with me, I knew... He knew. He knew what I was facing, and He held my hand the whole time. In every need, He got me a Five Star blessing.

Believing in and living with a Five Star God is what I consider a Well Life. I started that hash tag many years ago on social media for many reasons. I wanted to promote from overall health to a Well Life spiritual life. We can have a Well Life with God, but I do believe to live a Well Life, it takes some discipline and it's a form of art. Discipline by being disciplined to what's important to us, and an art by being creative and open to what is going to work in our own lives.

Well Life – A state of existence with God which includes enjoying the good health He wants us to have, an overall well-being, happiness, prosperity, attaining His wisdom, knowledge of our purpose, peace, abilities, and the gift of compassion so we may give of ourselves freely.

Discipline – To train to obey rules, a code of behavior, branch of knowledge, study higher education. Personal improvements. Better skills to personal growth.

Staying in God's presence at all times and in this present moment is a trained discipline and a very important one. Letting not one negative thought or word come out of our mouths is another trained discipline we can start working on today. Getting focused on what we want is a trained discipline and an art. We'll never see what we don't focus on.

Let that sink in a moment…we'll never see what we don't focus on…that's the truth in the natural and the spiritual worlds.

Shortly after moving to Florida, I slipped, tripped, and then fell in what was considered a very bad fall. With the slip and trip, my feet were lost to me, and I went full body weight down on my knee, hip, and palm of my hand and then continued a full body slip and slide coming down on my armpit flat. It was a crazy fall and put me into almost two years of healing, surgeries, and healing some more. That said, I was planning on finishing this book by December of that year. But I was in so much pain, I couldn't type or do anything with my right arm for any length of time. The aches and nerve pain made it impossible for me, "thus, no book work for me."

Now, zooming ahead two years, something bad that happened in my life that gave me more time to be in, what I like to call, 'boot camp for finishing this book,' my Five Star God showed me a few more very important lessons that would make this book even better in the end. I went through three major surgeries, tons of physical therapy, and quite of bit of up and down during my recovery. My recovery was so intense that riding a bike, writing, painting, or going for a walk was near impossible on most days, and those are my favorite things to do in life. I had so much down time. I had to recoup from the surgeries; and from having to live a sedentary lifestyle during those times of healing, I went through even more unpleasant times. It was a vicious circle for me; but with God, it was a victorious one. It doesn't make sense to feel this way, right? Maybe not, but, it's exactly the way I felt. Through it all, God kept me safe, secure, and happy. He showed me bits of wisdom He wanted in the book that I hadn't experienced yet, and above all… it's all Him, His book, and His timing in my life.

I want to ask you to do this little test that God asked me. There's no wrong answer as this is only for us to feel what we are feeling inside while doing this.

1. Picture yourself praying and asking God for something you need. It can be anything you need at the moment. How do you feel when you're praying about a need or want? Take a few minutes to focus on how you're feeling while praying in this manner. Please take note now of how you felt while praying those needs.

2. Now, take a moment and worship God in anyway that's natural for you. This time just focus on Him and what's special about Him that you'd like to worship. You can look at the sky, sing, pray the word, or clap your hands… anything. Do that now and take note of how you feel while doing this. Take as long as you like here to get a good comparison between the two, and write down notes if necessary.

Let me share what God showed me during this comparison of asking for things in prayer and worship prayer. On the first question, I was actually surprised by my feelings deep inside of me. I know from the scriptures we are to pray our needs because we have not, because we ask not; and we're to tell God our desires of our heart. But when I prayed and asked for any needs that came to mind, my personal feelings inside me were not what I would want at all. I felt like I was fretting, worrying, trying to make something happen, and not full of faith at all. I was actually shocked what the root of the asking came from inside of me, and that was me full of doubt, fear, and concern. Could I have felt like this my whole life when I prayed needs? Do you?

On question number two, what a difference worshipping God! I felt powerful, bold, believing, full of faith, courageous, strong, happy, joyful, peaceful, loving, and more. When the Lord spoke to me to do this and then after doing this test myself, I felt He had something very powerful to show us concerning our Five Star life. Can you guess what that is?

In the Word of God, we read to worship Him in spirit and truth, worship Him always, worship with our mouth, dance, and raising of our hands--worship Him in song and on and on. Just by going by what I felt like doing, with this little test, I want to just always worship Him, knowing who He is. I did not like how only asking for things or feeling like I had to pray my list of needs made me feel. We do need to talk to the Lord about our needs, but I believe we need to have a two-way relationship. Being aware that He knows us better than we know ourselves can help the relationship. I want to change up my asking to worship and declaring that He can take care of all my needs because that's when we feel His strength, His joy, and His power. At least that's what happened to me, and if it happened to you, too, then let's get that guilt- and shame-free relationship going!

Guilt-free – No more remorse, shame, and feeling bad. To move on. Liberty from emotions that weigh us down.

Now, let's go back to the key of this book, the word deserve. Did some of us just have a problem doing the test because we are still fighting the feeling we don't deserve to even pray or worship? We need to reexamine this if we did because we could still be fighting this even after reading the wisdom from God in this book, and some of us could have had trouble doing the simple test above. If that was any of us, let's remind ourselves here again that the key to the feeling and the word deserve is that we don't deserve, can't do anything more to deserve, God loves us, and it's all about Him. We are His children and He wants to do this for us; He says we deserve, so we deserve. He made us righteous. He did it all, so we didn't have to. It was never what we would do; it was always what He would do.

Remember it is all God, about God, through God, and Him alone. We are made whole through Him! The pressure should be off of us truly. Look at everything with God, through His eyes, and take on every situation, job, and goal with Him at the helm, Him doing it, guiding us through it, walking with us through everything. His talents, His strength, and His power is doing it all. When we truly grasp this, it will change our lives; the pressure can disappear and the peace will come.

Back to just asking God for things in prayer and worshiping Him through our prayers. Picture this and see if you agree this could be a better way to pray and keep ourselves feeling the power that comes from worshipping. Jesus told us to not be like the people repeating words over and over again, thinking, He'll hear us more or don't pray out loud in front of crowds showing off that we're spiritual. When you look at the "do's and don'ts," in the Lord's Prayer, I see some simple advice from above. It goes right along with what the Lord was showing me in the difference of how I felt in some of the stages I thought of prayer. Worshipping Him for who He is and acknowledging that loyalty in our relationship with Him, knowing He knows what we need, giving Him our weaknesses to take care of, following the path He has for us, and lifting all that right back up to Him in worshipping prayer is powerful and freeing. It is powerful because we are worshipping the God of the Universe and freeing because while He meets us in worship, we can talk to Him and hear

Him. We can worship and discuss everything we need to with Him because He has drawn near; and once we are in His presence, the confidence will come to ask our Father anything we need to ask without the enemy of our souls deferring us in doubt and guilt.

After this manner therefore pray ye: Our Father which art in heaven, Hallowed be thy name. Thy kingdom come, Thy will be done in earth, as it is in heaven. Give us this day our daily bread. And forgive us our debts, as we forgive our debtors. And lead us not into temptation, but deliver us from evil: For thine is the kingdom, and the power, and the glory, forever. Amen. ~ Matthew 6:9-13

But a time is coming and has now come when the true worshipers will worship the Father in spirit and in truth, for the Father is seeking such as these to worship Him. God is Spirit, and His worshipers must worship Him in spirit and in truth. ~ John 4:23-24

Our prayer lives will all be individual, of course, with our own relationship with God; our personalities are different, and each of our relationships with God will be unique also. But I hope each of us has a revelation here of a better understanding of what we can have with God. We don't want our own prayer lives to beat us up with worry and fretting. We don't want our prayer lives to be a Debbie Downer; we want to have an abundant Five Star life with our Heavenly Five Star God.

This is not to say we can't cry unto God or be broken before Him as there are times of prayer like that, and they are wonderful times before God. Useful too, we could be carrying a burden for someone in prayer or the Spirit is praying for what we don't even know ourselves. This is not what I'm referring to in the above paragraph. Please don't mix this up, because a healthy, balanced life will have both. When not heavy with a burden that God has asked us to carry in prayer, then we should let our prayers go up positive in faith and not fretting nor worry.

When we are feeling frustrated, not in control, or we don't see us ever having a solution for a need, then we can be sure we are looking at things through our human ability and reasoning; we are not looking at how big our God is and how He is able to find a way to take care of anything and everything for our good. We really do forget how much He loves us and cares for us, and His love is not based on if we think we deserve or not. Faith in God is the key and trust in God's ability to do so. It's all about Him, up to Him, and through Him. Take the pressure off yourself and put it back on God where it needs to be. He really does want to be loved and needed by us. We are not weaklings by any means, and we don't have to walk around in a weak mentality, but our strength comes from above, and we are strong in the Lord Jesus Christ, our Savior.

It's day by day--taking all the pressures off of us and giving them back to God. Even as I write this book, I'm fighting self-doubt and fretting about picking up my circumstances and doing something about my needs myself. So, this is truly a daily reminder to give it all to God, worship and talk to Him, and let Him help us.

God wants to be with us all day, every day. When things seem off, we think He pulled back, and then we usually go off on our own, not understanding what's happening. This is when we jump up in His lap and stay there safe under the wings of the Almighty. Let Him do it. Spending the day with God is simply taking Him with us, seeing through His eyes, talking with Him, and allowing His voice to minister and lead us. There are times we will want to get away from it all and spend real alone time with God, and that is wonderful; but He is with us in the car, while we are doing the dishes, and on our walks. Look out at the great, big world through His eyes and enjoy it with Him.

Take off the coat of shame and put on the coat the Lord has for you, and that's a coat of love and many colors. There is no shame in Him. Replace fretting with praise, and worry with worship. Scared? Believe in His protection. Change fear knowing His security. Discouraged? Be filled with peace!

We need to just go with God, not a set plan or our way on how it's supposed to happen. Be more open to how He will make it all work out. He will bless us in ways we can't fathom. He will send financial blessings other ways than our normal pay. He will send wisdom when we need it. He will guide us to the path we're to take. He will bring light to the darkness in our lives.

> *Process to the promise… we can misunderstand the processes of God in our lives, missing the promises.*

Process - procedure, an action, a series of actions or steps taken in order to achieve a particular end.

Promise - a declaration or assurance that one will do a particular thing or that a particular thing will happen.

The steps in our lives can be discouraging at times, but are they allowed to have a greater achievement? Does something not work out the way we want it because God has something better for us? Did we lose a job because there is a better one out there for us? This is how we need to process some of what we think is a loss or failure. God wants the best for us, so sometimes He does what I call, the "bur under the saddle." He upsets something to get us to move onto something better because of His promises!

Fear will actually get us to walk away or buck against the answers we need. Remember that God sees every one of us and hears our every prayer. Walking side by side with God, turning His promises into positive thinking, will help each of us feel powerful in Him. When we claim this, the process to the promise is possible and not out of reach for each of us.

If we knew all of His Five Star saves or miracles in our lives, some that we aren't even aware of, I think it would be extremely shocking to us. He is there, in our lives, in so many ways. God is not the genie in the sky, holding a two-by-four ready to hit us, in case we don't rub the magic jar right. His Five Star blessings are ours because He loves us and we are His children. He fixes relationships, performs miracle healings and financial miracles, provides jobs, and takes care of matters of the heart. He fixes them so well; I do believe most of the times we notice, we are wondering how He did it.

Five Star God is taking the matters of the heart that could hurt us and making them okay. We may come through something a little rough around the edges, but we're okay. We made it through when we may not have made it at all.

The matters of the heart can be mysterious obstacles in our lives. If there are matters of the heart in our lives that we don't know what to do with, the Lord can heal and remove them. He can give us Five Star wisdom during our hardest times even with our relationship with Him; and what's so wonderful about the Lord is that He will do this even when we are angry, feel fearful, and gone off alone on an island unto ourselves. Take a moment and call upon Him, and let's see

Five Star God

what happens! We will stop noticing how weak or strong we feel, because we will make Him our focus. Five Star is what we have available in our God and what He wants for us.

So, are you ready to look for, learn from, and get to know your Five Star God? Jesus is His name, and He's waiting to spend the day with YOU!

Reflection Questions –

What does it take to see Five Star God in our daily lives?

How does "asking only" make you feel in prayer?

How does worshipping and talking with God make you feel?

Do we look ahead a year or is it day by day?

thank you

I want to extend my sincerest thanks to the following people:

Randy Turner	Karen Ricci
Nathan Hayes	Linda Allen
Athena Tapuro Hurn	Kirk Tyler
Sherry Jackson Schneider	Sue Karoub
Carrie Hinchcliff Frye	Arielle Karoub
Emily Kramer	Bill Zurbrugg
Lyn Compau	Mekeisha Black
Vivian Gabrielly Meza	Cheri Shrock
KcLynn Fly	Dana Berisha
Darla Driggers	Rhonda Jones
Kelly Tanis	Dana Berisha
Stacey Graham Buher	Cyndy Lopez
Lynn Twilling	Kalpana Satyavolu
Diana Brown	Lianna D'angelo
Michele Kollig	Anna Kronsperger Kirk
Dorothy Karoub	Karla Gower
Elizabeth Gilbert	Coleen Blumhardt
Karyn Helder	Jeannie Peeper
Ada Bowman	Sherry Winn
Scott Karoub	Lisa Reister
Souleigha Shaw	Dawn Shew
Dennis Dingeldey	Valeria Hollaran
Cheri Riechers	Helen Mitchell
Sandy Hopper	Rachel Karoub
Kris DeKleine	Margo Dill

from the author

Thank you for reading Five Star God. I hope this book has blessed you the way it did for me. Day by day, I remind myself of His goodness, and I stand a little taller when it dawns on me He's with me in all things. Remember nothing is beyond God's reach, and no one is too far from Him that He won't hear your voice.

I love hearing from you!
www.ginaeleescott.com
Instagram @artistginae

about the author

Ginae Lee Scott is an artist and author of several books. Mom to three wonderful grown children, Ginae and her husband enjoy beaches, biking, and family time. Ginae works full time in her art studio and writes in her spare time. She loves to hear from her readers. She writes for you! Contact her at www.ginaeleescott.com

global giving initiative

As we pursue our mission to help people get their voices and ideas out into the world, we at Unprecedented Press realize that others are concerned with more pressing needs. Finding creativity in every person is important work, but getting food, shelter, and dignity to individuals must come first. That's why Unprecedented Press donates a portion of book revenue to the Everyone Global Giving Initative whose goal is to meet the practical needs of individuals around the world and to share the love of Jesus. To learn more, visit *everyoneglobal.com*

Other titles from Unprecedented Press

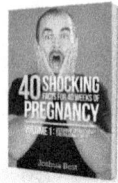

40 Shocking Facts for 40 Weeks of Pregnancy Volume 1- *Disturbing Details about Childbearing & Birth* By Joshua Best

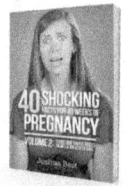

40 Shocking Facts for 40 Weeks of Pregnancy Volume 2 (*Terrifying Truths about Babies & Breastfeeding*) By Joshua Best

She Can Laugh - *A Guide to Living Spiritually, Emotionally & Physically Healthy* By Melissa Lea Hughes

Once Upon A Year - *Experience a year in the life of Finn* By Joanna Lenau

Y - Christian Millennial Manifesto
Addressing Our Strengths and Weaknesses to Advance the Kingdom of God By Joshua Best

Y, The Workbook - *A Companion*
By Joshua Best

Crumbs - *100 Everyday Stories about 100 People* By Rose White

The River - *A 30-day Study on the Role of the Holy Spirit in the Church, the World and you* By Mike Nicholson

Unstuck - *How to Grieve Well and Find New Footing* By Danette Johnson

Still Small Moments - *What Parenting Can Teach Us About Growing with God in Every Season* By April Best

Merbles - *A classic rags to rocky crags, to blue burndrops, to riches tale* By Matthew Kennedy

The Coffee Shop Gospel - *Where two or three are gathered...* By Dan Van Ommen

Landmarks - *A Comprehensive Look at the Foundations of Faith* By David Campbell

Half Everything - *The Curious Tale of a Creative Creature* By Joshua Best

Indispensable - *Small stories are worth telling* By Heidi Sugden

---

All titles available from Amazon.com or from UnprecedentedPress.com

www.ingramcontent.com/pod-product-compliance
Lightning Source LLC
Chambersburg PA
CBHW071211070526
44584CB00019B/2993